hymn to the heart

AKSHU

hymn to the heart

Copyright © 2023 Akshu

Made with ❤ on the Notion Press Platform

www.notionpress.com

For all the dreaming hearts who found their place among words.

Chapters

1. Reminiscence of yesterday

2. Ballad of a night owl

3. Letters of love

4. Point of view

5. Melody of a day dreamer

6. Hope of tomorrow

reminiscence of
yesterday

pen in my hands
bleeds,
memories of my nights and hope of my coming
days

you hear my laughter
can't you hear my silent screams?
echoing my thoughts
haunting my dreams

rising panic
it's hard to breathe
i find myself crying
eyes burning, my soul dying

they don't know how it feels
to wake up daily with nothing you could do
locked up in your mind's asylum
your anxiety and you

i am a stained cloth
with the imprints of you all over me
no matter how many times i wash myself
i'll never be completely clean
to me it's the reminder of your ugliness
but to others, it's unseen

~ SA diaries

 i opened our private folder today
pictures and videos of us lit up the screen
but before my eyes could see any
i deleted them all
call me cruel for erasing our memories
the last parts of your presence
because the reminder of you hurts more than
your absence

i sing my sorrow to the winds
hoping,
when they touch your skin
you feel the chills of my pain in your bones

today, i took the blade
sharp edges tracing my face
I'm screaming
not because of pain
i can't even cry
tears burn my cuts like acid rain
blood runs down my chin,
dripping on the floor
my demons knocking the door

shadows of fear surround me, i can't see
i hear my soul in darkness
echoing, Help Me. Help Me.

~ self harm

maybe my stars fell because they couldn't carry
the weight of your expectations

17

Eyes never called me pretty
but a Heart did

a walk in the woods
i saw the magic faraway tree
a portal to different worlds
home to the fairytale creatures

i took a climb to the top
and saw the land of forgotten
everything you ever lost would be here
and i searched everywhere
every street, every corner
but couldn't find it
i felt a tap on my shoulder
'what are you looking for?' asked a little elf
my voice came as a helpless whisper
'Myself'

Love, Loss, Pain, Regret
the cycle never ceases
you shot my glass heart
now it rest in pieces

they're under the spotlight
i hide behind the stage
they became a beloved book
i remained in the very first page

they had bigger goals
so i gave up my dream
they became a magnificent ocean
and i was a forgotten stream

i killed my childhood
so they could grow happy and free
mama, papa, they got everything
but what about me

~ eldest child

11:11
i hope i see you again,
 not in the stars
but wrapped in my arms
away from this place where no one can hurt us

Dear Moon,
are you the lonely child
in the classroom full of stars?
do the cool planets call you names?
do you get bullied by the mars?
does the big sun hate you? hate you for your
beauty or your scars

Dear Moon,
are you suppose to shine for others too?
did you grow up on your own?
was there no one to look after you?
do they light up your dark nights?
listen to your pain, like you always do

Dear Moon,
was this universe welcoming?
does it ever cared for your being?
did you never felt belonged?
or do you change phases just to fit in

Dear Moon,
are you the lonely child in the place full of stars?
are you like me?
someone watching from afar

" what am I too you " he asked

" you are the poetry beating in my heart, you've
been in here longer than I remember. And even if
one day it stops, you'll still be here, living like an
old tale. Forever " I replied

i'm learning to worship the goddess between my
legs before i let him to do so

25

little being of feathers
aiming for the sky
won't even jump
afraid to fall and die

little being of feathers
watch others fly
hides in the willows
and cry

yesterday my brother fell down
while playing
scraped his knee, blood came running
i called my mother, she told him not to cry
that this was a test of bravery
sign of a mighty soldier
mark of a pride holder
shouldn't be ashamed of it, never

today it was me bleeding
not from the knee but from between my legs
i didn't cry, like a brave soldier i was
but when i told my mother, she shushed me out
that it's not a warrior stain
it is a womanhood pain
i shall never speak of it again
should be ashamed of it forever

go chase the stars
not the ones that decides your destiny
but the ones you wish and dream upon

she had an argument
with man she calls her love
he raised his voice
and she shrunk down
arms wrapped around as an armor
his love took a step back, confused
on the sight of her
trembling like a little kid she was once

~ childhood trauma

my words do scream
louder than any of their actions

~ a poet

keep your head low
stay quiet
the world is a hunter's trap, you survive
only if you play right
cover your limbs, avoid their preying eyes or
become one
that's the circle of life
one mistake and you're done

~ *guidelines for women*

wasn't it easy
back
when the playground
was your second home
home work
was your sworn enemy
high shelves,
you couldn't reach without an
elder's help
when the world was only in textbooks
not the one you live in now

tomorrow is scary, especially with
the reminders of yesterday's hauntings
growing up does not excites
when the little kid in you is still hurting

loving again isn't easy
 when your heart is still collecting pieces,
will to go on shatters
when your life is hanging on creases

so tell me,
how i am suppose to see the coming
daylight
when my eyes are all blinded by the
night

i plucked all my thorns
the flowers bloomed from my scars
i collected the red ink dripping from
my pricked fingers
and wrote *a hymn to my heart*

the one who has seen it all
the one who knows it all

37

ballad of a night owl

so lost
in this human race
left behind, tore apart
can't find my true face

so sick
of picture perfect good
either be flawless
or hide under the hood

so tired
of carrying your expectations
pushing my limits
crushing my patience

so bored
of this status game
faking myself
for the name of fame

so stupid
trying to be something pure
in this tainted world

i tried
and tried
sorry but i couldn't survive it

i died
and died
in the dark ocean i dived in

the monsters are crawling up
even
the angels can't save me

i have become the one
i wasn't suppose to be

bird of air
with no wings to fly

skin on her skin
it was hard to breathe
those hands on her
harsh, burning seethe
she screamed, she cried
but nobody heard her pain
and they didn't stopped
doing it again and again

that beautiful fragile body was shattered into
pieces
torn inside out, left for her demise
dead tears shedding from her eyes
they left nothing behind, except for one thing
Fear,
fear that the next girl would be me
fear that she'll die if i set her free
fear that'll live forever in her heart, that there is a
monster outside ready to tear her apart
fear that she won't be able to survive
fear that she'll die despite being alive

they call me a *fool*
they think i'm *insane*
a lone flower wilting in *pain*
cuz, oh honey
they know
that i'll risk everything
just to hold you in my arms
again

who wants peace when one can be *fanaa*,
destroyed in love

you were like a dream
made of stardust
a charming, mystic soul
like an enchanted forest, too beautiful to trust

every touch felt celestial and rare
every kiss was a soulful prayer

you built us a home
with all the magical love spells
you somehow heard my coins, i flipped
in all those wishing wells

but a dream isn't real, i realized

every touch became withered
every kiss came cursed
crack on the wall and magic burst

love was crushed, like a flower
soft and frail
alas, it was my fault
for falling in love with a *fairytale*

Sun, who burned for him
Moon, who loved her from afar
two longing hearts, separated by day and night
stole glances at golden hour
but once a year their paths collide
coalesce of souls and touch of lips
celestial love, *Eclipse*

amber eyes
fierce sight
fiery wings
burning throughout the flight

~ *she is a phoenix*

at last human was more transparent
than water

i stared at the night sky, for a little too long
the moon sighed and asked
'what is their name'

you were like a wave of colours
in my parched grey life

summer nights
we sneaked out of our homes
to the place in the woods,
we once marked our own
those love filled eyes, soft lips on my skin you
were the only love i had ever known

young and naïve
us facing the world, like two little birds flying in
the stormy skies
to have a beautiful future in our hands
a hopeless day dream in our innocent eyes

now that time is long gone
you are not here anymore
but the reminder hits back eyerytime
like waves to the shore

cause here i am again
back to our secret woodland
with an injured heart inside
and dead love's ashes in my hands

our stolen prayer
we were there

I still see it, *all too well*

Maa,
i'm walking on a tightrope
if i fall
catch me before the world does

reading is my escapism
writing is my coping mechanism

i remember our first kiss
it was a total disaster
how your lips accidently touched mine while fixing
my window sill
the growing age, the newness of doing things was
a different kind of thrill

i remember our second kiss
the core memory of my life
how your touch made me forgot all the other
doubts
i felt like the girl i used to read in books about

i remember our last kiss
never thought we'd have one
how you climbed off my balcony
saying, i'll see you tomorrow
days passed, i still wait there
with eyes full of hope and heart full of sorrow

i find *heaven* in between your arms
but when you're in between my legs,
it feels as if i found my *salvation*

when the words on that sheet hits you like an
arrow of lightning, you feel its thunder in your
blood and bones, the crackle of those lines echoes
in your soul, words piercing your heart, leaving a
beautiful wound and when its ache stays forever

that's what poetry feels like

i hold the quill in my hand
ink of my life flows
flipping through the pages,
stopping at the chapter of yours

your name stormed in, unalarmed
flew up all my pages, swiped me off my feet
our story began, i was sitting on the first seat
watching us flying in love
over the fairytale we wrote together
the home of dreams we built together

but soon the weather changed for worst
the bubble of romance burst
i fell hard on the ground
flipped all the pages back
but couldn't turned it around
and
just like the storm, soon you were gone
quill still in my hand but the ink flows on

now i sit in the ruins
of place we once called home
flipping, waiting
for *story of us* to end
alone

an acolyte by heart
love is my only religion

she was the poet
he was her words
their love was a tragedy
unread, unheard
she kept it hidden in those folded inked pages,
inside the deepest corner of her heart

but one day, those pages flew away and the
tragedy became a wonder of
art

she carries the night sky in her dark hair
the sun drowns in her eyes
the earth gave its colour to her
 the crowd calls her goddess when she walks by
and
you have the audacity to call her ugly

~brown girl

how many times these thoughts
have kept me up all night
blaring harsh, as a stormy sea
and i can't help but let my ship sink in it

letters of love

Dear Diary,

there is this one girl i know
she likes books, music, chocolates,
plants especially flowers
the Disney, marvel universe
the night full of stars
sweet smell of rain, a child's laugh
painting on the walls
dancing bare feet
singing poetry in empty halls

she cry over little things
daydreams her fictional reality
a hopeless romantic
taylor swift is her entire personality

careless and crazy
loud and messy
wild and free

i know this one girl
who is just like me

with love
her

Dear Reader,

i tell you a story
of a feisty dreamer
my little red bird
she tried to sing them
but her voice was unheard
so she escaped into the gap between words

she inked her thoughts on
 a piece of paper

she wrote about
her shattered hopes, the stories
behind her scars
she wrote about
the war she fought, to change the fate
of her stars

she wrote about
her secret wishes, every coin of
dream she ever tossed
she wrote about
the ones she love
and the one she lost

she wrote about
her journey, every fallen step before
a new start

she wrote about
her experiences, from her first day of school
to the first time a boy broke her heart

she wrote about
the life lessons she learned
 in past years
she wrote about
the toughness she earned from thousand
shedded tears

she kept writing
letting it all bleed
hoping that one day her words would reach out to
someone in need
and that day new pages would be torn
that day a new writer would be born

with love
a little poet

Dear Love,

i am a girl who likes to read about you
think about you, write about you
they call me a hopeless romantic
because i hope my life to be like a
romance book

i wish to experience it all
from cute picnic dates
to dancing in a masquerade ball

from my first kiss in the rain moment
to walking down the stairs,
wearing the prettiest dress
searching for his eyes among
thousand stares

i want it all
cute nicknames and annotated books
love notes
hidden in my pocket
stolen glances and soft brushes
my picture in his heart shaped locket

i want it all
i want to read him my poetries
build a place in his heart to stay
from getting down on one knee
to dance on Ed Sheeran's 'perfect'
on our wedding day

i want it all
i hope of it all
i dream of it all

with love
her

Dear Girl,

it's okay if you don't wake up
with perfect skin and perfect hair,
don't worry about the meaningless comments
on the colour your skin wear
you don't have to blame yourself
because of some unwanted stares
don't have to be ashamed of those
extra curves and body hairs

i don't think those spots and marks
on your face are ugly, my dear
i know those insecurities might feel like
making yourself disappear
So
there is something i want you to hear

that *you are a piece of Art,*

unique and beautiful
made of vibrant colours, shades, and tones
different structure
and different texture
of skin and bones

each stroke of those beauty marks
are like galaxies of stars
the shining glow of ocean are those
minor details of scars

beautiful beyond false beauty comparison
that's what you are

with love
your sister

My Dear Angel boy,

i've been thinking about you a lot
lately
especially when i sit down to write
when i pass through your home
when our favorite ice-cream shop comes to sight

i look at the moon and think about
the grey of your eyes
i think about our secret jokes
when i see your smile in polaroids

i think about your warm hugs
in the cold winter nights
i think about our stolen kisses
under the street light

i think about you
when i hear our favorite song
i think about that tuesday where it all went wrong

i remember you laying on the bed made of woods
burning all our memories with you
and i stood there with teary eyes
my soul burning into ashes too

i never told anyone about you
you were a hidden secret in my heart
the beautiful boy who found his peace among
stars
but the time is long gone
and along with the winds i'm moving on

so this is my farewell to you
this is my closure to you
the goodbye we never had a chance to
i love you forever
i'll always do

with love
your girl

Dear Gardner,

in your garden of beauty
where love lives in its
soft scented air
courtesy is the ornament
each flower wear
where elegance flows in its murmuring water
nourishing the grass as its own daughter
where each plant is
a symbol of perfection
vines shows grace with every flexion

in this garden of beauty
she blooms among thorns
nourish among weeds
strength and fierceness
she wear them like beads

tangled and flawed
the one who is never picked
a wild creature
deserted by others and welcomed by nature

with love
a wild flower

point of view

i wish i could read me
through your point of view

1

i saw him today
tried my best not to care
he didn't even look at me but he knew
i was there
i walk past him
the ache of his touch, his voice, his love
grew with each step
every piece of my heart hoping for him to
stop me, tell me to stay
but he did nothing
so i simply walked away

1

i felt peace in the air
and my heart knew it was her
walking by
and my hand out of habit tried to reach out for
her
beg her to stay
but the wall between us was too strong
ugly reminder of our past wrongs
so i stood there
with a heavy heart
watched you walking away, forever

2

the boy with sun in his eyes
the golden warmth of my day
doesn't know, that his laugh heals
me in every possible way
a beautiful ray of light
miles away from darkness of my heart
could ever love me?

2

she is the quiet moon among
million shimmering stars
her eyes hold untold stories
i want to read all of them
i want that guarded heart of hers
i want to hold her close, never let her fall
i want to love her, with everything i am

3

i heard the shattering first
then saw those crystal wounds in your eyes
pieces that i left for you
i'm sorry my beautiful boy
i couldn't give a reason to your why
you poured your heart in my hands
and i crushed it with a goodbye

3

i'm still holding on the pieces
the sand hasn't moved since the storm
the glass cuts my skin
but my eyes are fixed on your footprints
walking away from me
still waiting, still hoping
so when the run is over and you have nowhere
else to be
remember, i will be there
right where you left me

4

you were the burning red
i was the midnight blues
the sky was our battle field
the morning blush
against
the after rain shield

4

after years of weathering
storming out
heavens and ground
a thunder named love
struck us back
and painted our sky
lilac

5

it's tiring, even for history
to be this repetitive
each rose you offered
from the garden of your mistakes
each time i accepted them,
it breaks more than it mends
you say, *i'm sorry*
i say, *i forgive you*
the cycle never ends

5

i am sorry.

6

i hear your laugh
in the hallway and everything stops
one small talk
and i'm struck with a whirlwind in my heart
an ephemeral moment that left a
permanent mark
now you captivate my thoughts
just like stars glimmering the dark
and all i do
is to wish for my name
to not get blurred in your memory
i wish you to think about
the stolen glances during corridor strolls
the lunch break chaos, the red ribbon
the girl in painted white tee
i wish you think about me

6

each time i close my eyes
and think about my backpack days
i'm filled with yearning, in a shape of
red ribbon and a blurry face
i cut it out
i know it's for my own best
lock in my mind but this stupid heart of mine
wont rest, louder
than the crowd outside
the thoughts i'm trying to avoid
somehow all comes back to that voice
to that moment
stolen from a film reel
from the first hello to the last goodbye
all in one scene
all the what ifs
about what could have been mine
i think about her, all the damn time

melody of a daydreamer

my heart was a wanderer
living in an endless world
like a broken jewelry of dull stones
and solitude pearled
but
the day i met you
i felt an anticipation
cause i heard my heart whispering
'honey we found our destination'

little human,
who had their entire life planned as a kid
now search for a reason to live

you painted my canvas RED
the colour that never fades

stars collide
heavenly sight
oceanic blues meets the dark night

~ *eye contact*

and just like the waters,
her mind is restless
home to many thoughts
some hidden in its depth and
some waiting to be pulled out

i am not a child
i am an experimental project
i redesign and upgrade myself
every time
so they could be satisfied
i work beyond my limits
even it deteriorates me, i keep going.
i am not allowed to feel anything
i function as they command
because that's what i was made for
but
now it scares me
what if one day my system crashes
my battery dies permanently
would it be my fault
or someone else to blame for

the power,
those small four letter words hold
one brings the world together and other breaks it
into million

~ *Love and Hate*

i almost didn't believed
when you said, 'it was fun'
took a moment to realize
again the other woman
never the one

my eyes up there, talking to you
retelling the old times in every possible way
i can still hear your giggles
even if you're miles away
caught you blushing, golden red
on something i say
clicking a picture of you, cuz honey
you look beautiful today

~ *flirting with the sky*

the connection between me and nature
runs deeper than any verse of poetry
i befriended soil when i was a kid,
spending my entire day cuddling with it
i grew up listening
to the songs of mountains,
the music of river waters
i grew up reading tales of enchanted forests, living
among the lives found there
it's like
my heart is tangled
with every root on the ground
it feels me, it heals me and when
it calls me
i hear it in my skin and bones
my soul demands me to run free
and when i'm there,
it feels like
coming home

cut open a poet's heart
it will bleed *love*

dear girl,
there is a fire raging inside you
bright enough to light up the
whole town
fierce enough to burn it all down

you must have left us for a reason
leaving all the mess for me to clean
broken bottle on the kitchen floor
my splattered heart stains unseen

when the
string of red got slashing
ugly words came crashing
your sign on papers flashing
champagne problems

our love on blaze, i watch it
lighter in your hand, i couldn't stop it
you called it quit and i called it
champagne problems

i want to seize
all the beats your heart skips
whenever *we touch*

if spring was a person
it would be you

i live in this place

where
happy faces are framed on the walls
covering the cracks of sorrowful bawls

where
love is served in a lavish dinner
that taste like poison under all that shimmer

where
others are treated with all the love
and affection
but some with cold words and abusive
actions

i live in this place
that screams
RUN
they call it a *Home*
but doesn't feel like one

~ *toxic household*

'what do we fight for'

' Power. Vengeance. Love '

taste of power and hunger of vengeance is what
we live for, bleed for. Love is just an old myth,
dead and buried in books

dear beautiful soul,

it is somewhere out there,
like a lost poetry
and one day its words will make a way to you
its music will beat in your hearts
and life would be meaningful

regards,
love

i miss your warm hugs
your quartz eyes
your soft arms
holding me all night

when i said its time
to leave me behind
but you stayed
proved me wrong and our love right

maybe this is me blind hoping
the little thread of faith i'm holding
if i could change our stars,
i swear i'm ready to fight

i would have you back again
but i can't
so if the night dark and cold
i understand

so this is me wilting my life
pricking my heart,
lost the only thing that was mine

eachtime, winds take me
back to that December night

dear love,
you are a kind of chaos i want in my life
forever

my body is a temple
and you my priest, worship it
with passion
love me as something
sacred and rare
i hear my name on your tongue
a hymn, a beautiful prayer

this love is our religion
this is how we pray
this is our salvation

our love became an old tale
the future we talked about became
our history
now you are just a lost chapter
of my life
folded in the corners of my
memories

dust in the haunting air
of the blue abandoned room
nobody stepped in for 12 moons
unmade bed, clothes on the chair
polaroids on the wall
half wrapped birthday present still lays there

in the room that got frozen in time

your scent like memories echoes
everywhere
the laughs and pain we shared
i collect them all like something fragile
and rare
and bury them in a cardboard box
i have cried ocean before
so i let this room a sole tear
one last glance, one last prayer

this is where it ends
this is where it stops
this is what i fear
that
i'll slowly forget the husk of your voice,
the grey of your eyes
love of my life

in the blue room
that'll always remain frozen in time

oh peter pan
hold my hand
fly me beyond the clouds
where life isn't just *a fairytale*

hope of tomorrow

my soul embraced
my body
and whispered
you are beautiful

life is outraging lately
but she is prepared
they are calling her names lately
but she doesn't care
'the skin shedding rattler'
no, a courageous adapter
'the ruins of city frames'
i see a rising bird of flames

they're throwing arrows and traps
to hunt her down
but she's the deadly lioness
who rules the ground

so bring it all
weapons of
hatred, anger, jealousy
but she won't fall

they said
write your heart out
but
all it knows is pain
and
oh reader, *pain is contagious*

broken armour
and we are free
healing together
you and me

it took some years
but now i can finally laugh at your
name
instead of shedding tears

~ *moving on*

one day
i closed my eyes and saw a girl who
lived an invisible life
one day
i broke off her worldly ties
slashing them off with a blunt knife
she laughed
she cried
told me the story,
how she lived
ignored and terrified

but now her fears were gone
she was free from the ground
growing and glowing
glad to be found

one day
i closed my eyes
and let my soul see
that day
i shut the world out
and
saw me
only *me*

i have become the Roar
of every muffled cry
in my bloodline

~ *today's daughter*

now i'm wrapped in your arms again
miles away from yesterday's pain
and you my awaited love
were singing in my ear

it ends here
and we are the new beginning, my dear

home is not a place
no four walls, no roof
it's the warmth of their arms
love in their laughs
where you smile too

~ comfort people

tonight
we all cousins sat by the fireplace
talking and laughing
when my elder said
'tell me what you all achieved today'

one by one they all spoke
'i stood first at the school race'
'boss was impressed, i got a pay raise'
'i won that critical case'
'finally bought a new place'

they all shared their winning
now it was turn to say
i smiled with happy moist eyes
'i ate all my meal today'

~ *ed journey*

two sides of the story

the one inside the inked sheets
and the one holding the quill

one day her name
would be written on the walls
for them to remember her,
for him to worship her

gone is the season of rosy cheeks
warm socks and frosty nights
cheers to the season of dandelions
baby leaves and longer daylight

end of the year book
beginning of a new chapter

with you
each day is the love day
no matter what calendar says

~ 14 february

i create beauty each time
i break
head line of every whisper you
make
i'm a poisoned truth in your sweet lies
so wreck me once
wreck me twice
even in that melancholia
i cry diamonds from my eyes

i'm the understanding one
the listener
because they talk and i listen
they take my quietness as silence
so my voice gets buried somewhere in
the conversations

i'm the easy child
the mature one
who grew up before time to be
the carrier of their expectations

i'm the tired one
always at the verge of breaking
always trying too hard
because the voices in my head screams,
'you will never be good enough'

i'm the lost one
the one who never belonged
struggling to adjust my little soft heart
in this world so rough and wrong

how many roles
i play at a time
unaware of what i feel inside,
what i truly want to be

how many more
versions
it would take, for them
to see the real me

until then,
i'll continue to be the one

____

sand slips from the hour glass
slowly at a pace
till the last particle falls

then the maker flips it back
and the cycle repeats

~ *life*

i intertwine my heart
with every other person
who gives me the slightest affection
even if it means nothing to them
maybe,
it's the love starved kid in me to blame for

we might not share the same blood
we might not have same hair
or same eyes
but my heart has always called her sister

~ *female friendship*

" you have the most beautiful eyes "
he said

" they are just brown, what could be special about
brown eyes? "
 i asked

" eyes like golden skies, as if they have
drowned the sun in them
eyes that reminds me of sweetness of
honey, ambery warmth of love
eyes like dark woods, to be lost and
never found
eyes like burning stars, like mysteries
of universe, yet to be discovered
eyes worth loving and dying for "
he replied

i am
disconnecting the rest of the world
to reconnect with myself
blocking all my 'what ifs'
i have
decided to follow my heart

a heart to give
a life to be live
a soul to be kind
and
a peaceful mind

in the end, that's what matters

air in the room gets contagious
with my presence
each rose we planted now
withers with my sadness
everyone is leaving the mess
i have become
now all i'm left with the ghosts
of my madness

i reached for them
found the closed door at my face
alone in dark
standing start of this mental race
i ran for my life
fell, bleed, defeat, repeat
didn't stop
until i became the light

to the eyes
for choosing this book
to the hands
for flipping through the pages
to the heart
for feeling my words

~ a big thank you

END WORD

My first thought while writing this book was that
it's no longer just me, my pen and my diary.
People are actually going to read it.
My second thought was that nobody is gonna
read it, but here we are.

 Writing has always been my coping mechanism, i
spend half of my day flipping through empty
pages, feeling all the emotions and bleeding it all
out on a paper. I started writing poetry when i
didn't even knew what poetry was. Some called it
a beautiful collection of words, some said what i
write is not poetry because they have a
misconception that poetry is just a jumble of
gigantic and complicated words, too difficult to
understand
     but isn't poetry what makes life easy and
understandable, isn't it what uncomplicates
everything

i write poetry because it makes everything simple.
i write poetry because it makes me *Feel,* feel the
ecstasy of love, agony, happiness, hurt, anger but
most importantly *heard.* I write for the invisible
ones, the quiet ones, the lonely ones, the lost
ones and for the people who guard their

emotions, who locks up the turmoil in their hearts because they feel that nobody will understand them.
I hear you. I feel you. I understand you.

I write because i found my voice in those written words and maybe one day these words would become someone else's voice.
 Hymn to the heart is that voice, disguised as a dream, a dream that i chased, a dream to have my own place among the world of words

I found mine, i hope you find yours too.

About the writer

she tries to be that quiet mysterious girl but she always got something loud to write

you can contact her on
https://www.instagram.com/akshuwritess
akshuwrites03@gmail.com